Kevin and the Answer Machine

written by Angelica Corcoran & Abishek Muralikrishna

Kevin and the Answer Machine

ISBN: 979-8-9944990-4-7

Independently published · First edition, 2026

Printed in the United States of America by Amazon KDP.

Kevin looked out his window and wondered.

"What will I be when I grow up?"

An inventor? A scientist? An animal helper?

So many dreams to choose from.

At school, his teacher had big news.

"Make something that helps someone. The best projects go in the school showcase!"

Kevin felt excited. And a little wobbly inside.

"What if my idea isn't good enough?" Kevin whispered.

His teacher smiled.

"Every great invention starts as a not-good-enough idea."

That night, Kevin stared at a blank piece of paper.

The paper stared back.

Dad peeked in. "Have you tried asking the Answer Machine?"

"The what?"

"Some people call it AI. It mixes together ideas from all the people who ever wrote things down. It's very clever."

Dad grinned. "But it's not always right. Remember that."

Kevin typed his first question:

How can kids help make the world better?

Ideas filled the screen. Help animals! Protect nature! Build things! Teach others!

It wasn't an answer. It was a starting point.

The next day, Kevin saw his neighbor Mrs. Chen wobbling up her steps, arms full of groceries.

An apple rolled. Then an orange.

Ding! An idea.

Kevin burst through the front door.

"Dad! I'm going to build something that carries heavy things!"

Kevin started typing: *My neighbor Mrs. Chen lives at*

"Whoa there," said Dad gently. "We never tell the machine people's private things. Names, addresses, secrets, those belong to people."

Kevin nodded and typed instead: *How can I help a neighbor carry groceries?*

The Answer Machine had LOTS of ideas.

Carts. Wagons. Pulleys.

And one idea in big, confident letters:

BALLOONS CAN LIFT HEAVY GROCERIES!

"Balloons!" gasped Kevin. "Of course!"

Kevin huffed and puffed until he'd blown up twelve balloons. He tied them to a basket of apples.

The basket did not lift. The basket did not budge.
It tipped right into the rose bush.

POP. POP. POP-POP-POP.

"But the machine sounded SO sure!" said Kevin.

Dad laughed kindly. "The Answer Machine always sounds sure, even when it's wrong. That's why inventors check."

He tapped Kevin's head. **"Ask it. Check it. Test it. Make it yours."**

So Kevin checked with real people.

He asked Mrs. Chen. He asked his teacher. He asked the mail carrier, the crossing guard, and Mr. Ruiz, who rolls to the market in his wheelchair.

Everyone had a different problem to carry.

And that's when Kevin understood.

He didn't want to build a cart.

He wanted to help Mrs. Chen.

Kevin used the machine to sketch ideas. To organize his notes. To find out how wheels work.

But every idea got the Kevin Test:

Ask it. Check it. Test it. Make it yours.

Some ideas flopped. The wheels wobbled. The handle snapped.

"How's it going?" asked Dad.

"Test it," said Kevin. "Test it again." He grinned. **"I'm learning."**

Then one morning, it rolled.

The Helper Cart!

With big soft wheels for bumpy sidewalks, a low shelf Mr. Ruiz could reach from his wheelchair, and a little fold-out ramp for Mrs. Chen’s steps.

Showcase day.

Kevin's invention wasn't the biggest. It wasn't the fanciest.

But it solved real problems, for real people.

"Did a computer make this?" a judge asked.

Kevin shook his head. "The machine helped me look. But I asked the questions. I checked the answers. I tested every piece."

"The ideas that worked are mine."

"Kevin — the Big Ideas Award!"

Everyone clapped. Kevin's ears went hot, and his smile went wide.

But the best part came after.

Mrs. Chen unfolded the little ramp, and the Helper Cart rolled right up her steps, easy as anything.

"You saw me," she said. "You helped me."

That night, Kevin looked up at the stars.

He didn’t feel wobbly at all.

So many dreams still waiting to be built.

And Kevin knew just how to build them.

With wondering. With courage. With hard work.

And with a machine that helps,

as long as you remember:

ASK

CHECK

TEST

MAKE IT YOURS

Ask it. Check it.
Test it. Make it yours.

The End.

For Grown-Ups

Five things Kevin knows about AI (and your child can too)

- **AI is made by people.** It mixes together ideas people already wrote down. It doesn't have dreams of its own.
- **AI can be wrong, even when it sounds sure.** Just like the balloons! Always check important answers with a grown-up, a book, or a test.
- **AI can be right, too.** The machine also suggested carts and pulleys, good ideas Kevin used. The trick isn't "never trust it." The trick is "always check it."
- **Private things belong to people.** Never tell AI your name, address, school, or secrets.
- **AI is a tool, not a friend.** Friends are people (and pets!). A machine doesn't know you, it just follows patterns.

Talk about it together

- The machine told Kevin balloons could lift groceries. Why do you think it was wrong?
- What does Kevin mean when he says "the ideas that worked are mine"?
- Kevin's dad stopped him from typing Mrs. Chen's address. What things should we keep private from computers?
- Kevin asked real people about their problems. Why did that work better than only asking the machine?
- The Helper Cart has a low shelf for Mr. Ruiz and a ramp for Mrs. Chen. How did listening give Kevin better ideas?
- If you could invent something to help someone you know, what would it be? (Try the Kevin Test: Ask it. Check it. Test it. Make it yours!)

A note on age

Best shared as a read-aloud for ages 4–6 and independent reading for 6–8. The refrain is designed for kids to chant along by the second read.

THE KEVIN TEST

Ask it.
Check it.
Test it.
Make it yours.

for every big idea, from a machine or anywhere else

About the creators

Abishek Muralikrishna teaches clever Answer Machines how to help people think, learn, and build amazing things. Angelica Corcoran loves bringing people together, spreading kindness, and helping everyone feel welcome. Together, they created Kevin to show that the biggest ideas come from curious minds, caring hearts, and a little courage. They hope this story encourages every child to imagine, invent, and make the world a little brighter.

www.ingramcontent.com/pod-product-compliance
Lightning Source LLC
LaVergne TN
LVHW070626061126
851857LV00002B/22
* 9 7 9 8 9 9 4 4 9 9 0 4 7 *